13345

CLARENCE DARROW

CLARENCE DARROW

A ONE-MAN PLAY

by

David W. Rintels

Produced by

Mike Merrick and Don Gregory

Based upon

Irving Stone's

Clarence Darrow for the Defense

12133

DOUBLEDAY & COMPANY, INC.

GARDEN CITY, NEW YORK

MIKE MERRICK and DON GREGORY present

HENRY FONDA
as
CLARENCE DARROW

a new play by
DAVID W. RINTELS

based on "Clarence Darrow for the Defense" by
IRVING STONE

scenery and lighting by
H.R. POINDEXTER

directed by
JOHN HOUSEMAN

production stage manager
GEORGE ECKERT

general manager
JAMES AWE

A DOME PRODUCTION

To Henry Fonda and
John Houseman,
teachers and friends.

CLARENCE DARROW

ACT ONE

The curtain is always up.

The stage has four distinct areas on four slightly different levels.

Downstage is a bare runway, close to the audience, for DARROW *"in one."*

Stage right is CLARENCE DARROW's *Chicago law office of the 1920s, spare and traditional. Desk and chair, an overstuffed couch for his friends and clients, a thin rug, a framed photograph of John Peter Altgeld competing for room on the desk with all the books and papers.*

Stage center, a courtroom. Upstage, dominating the stage, there is an elevated judge's bench joined to a witness box. They are bracketed by the 48-star flag and the flag of the state of Illinois. Downstage center, a defense table with two chairs for defendants and one for DARROW. *Left center is the suggestion of a jury-box-with-rail.*

The combined bedroom-living room of DARROW's *Chicago apartment of the late 1890s is at stage*

9

left. Two chairs, one a simple rocker, a bed, a gas reading lamp, a table, a wall of well-thumbed books, a window.

DARROW *was a warm, loving man, rumpled, comfortable, unceremonial. The far sides of the stage reflect that; all the majesty is in the courtroom in the center.*

A backdrop indicates the Chicago skyline of the 1920s.

DARROW *enters slowly from stage right. He is sixty-seven years old, a big man, leonine, with a tendency to slouch that concerns him not a bit. His long, graying hair is so carelessly combed it threatens constantly to obscure his right eye. He is wearing the same unpressed gray suit that he has worn for years, a shirt and tie without style.*

Coming through the courtroom he pauses to look at the defense table where Loeb and Leopold sat; the bench where Judge Caverly presided; the witness box where Bryan sat. In the same mood of remembering, he comes to the in-one area and begins.

DARROW:

When I was very young, not over seven or eight years old, my father told me about a murder that was committed when he was a young man. It happened in the town adjoining the one where we lived in Ohio. In those days, a murderer was hanged outdoors in broad daylight, and everyone was invited to see the act and all the gruesome details that went with it. It was an eager and anxious crowd, each pushing to be in at the moment of death. My father managed to get well in front where he could watch, but when he saw the rope adjusted around the man's neck he could stand no more. My father turned away his head and felt humiliated and ashamed for the rest of his life that he could have had that much of a hand in killing a fellow man.

(*Moving into the bedroom-living room*)

My father and mother were not usual people. They were freethinkers in a valley full of rock-ribbed religionists . . . the only Democrats among Republicans for as far as you could see . . . the only intellectuals. Would you believe my mother thought women should be allowed to vote—and even said so, right out loud, as early as 1840? And—I remember this perfectly, even though I was only seven or eight at the time—she never protested when my father kept me out 'til midnight riding with him on a hay wagon—

—because, buried under the straw, were slaves my father was helping to escape from south to north, from slavery to freedom, along the Underground Railway.

(*Fondly picking up a book*)

My father always did just enough work for hire—carpentry, house painting, driving a hearse—to be able to buy books. Hebrew, Greek, Latin, law, metaphysics, science, religion. He loved his books. He loved us to read them. If I became anything at all, I owe it to my father's patience and his books—

—and to be honest about it, to some plain hard work on my own part. When I was nine, my father set me to work on the hottest summer day I can ever remember, hoeing potatoes—

—and after I had worked hard for a few hours, I ran away from that hard work, went into the practice of law, and have not done any work since.

(Coming downstage)

Why the law? Well, in Kinsman on every fourth of July, when Squire Allen got through reading the Declaration of Independence, which we thought he'd written because he always read it, he introduced some lawyer from the county seat. I had seen the lawyer's horse and buggy at the hotel in the morning, and I thought how nice they were and how much money a lawyer must make. He never seemed a bit afraid to stand up before the public. I remember his boots looked shiny, as though they had just been greased. He talked very loud and waved his hands and arms a great deal. The old farmers clapped and nodded their heads and said, ". . . mighty smart man . . . great man."

That's why the law.

(Then, dead serious)

I've never been sure I made the right choice. The law is a bum profession as generally practiced. It's devoid of idealism, almost poverty-stricken as to any real ideals. But I only learned that when I was in too deep to get out. My trouble was, I was fascinated by the *idea* of the law—the clash of good minds, the people I'd meet. That was even better than baseball—although one afternoon in high school, with my girl friend Jessie watching, I came to bat in the last of the ninth with us one run down, two men on, two men out. Just like Casey at the Bat, only—

(*He wiggles into his stance*)

—I hit one over the grocery store to win the game. Nothing would ever be better than that.

Not even the Monkey Trial.

I didn't have much education. One year of college. One year of law school, in Ann Arbor. In those days a committee of lawyers examined you for admission to the bar. They were all good fellows and wanted to help you through. Today the Bar Association is about as anxious to encourage competition as the Plumbers' Union, or The American Medical Association. My first lawyer business was drawing up a contract for a horse trade. For this I was paid fifty cents—by each side. With all that cash jingling in my pockets, I felt so flush and reckless I asked Jessie to marry me. It made Jessie so reckless she decided to take a chance.

Prettiest girl you ever saw. Kindest, easiest-going, simplest in her tastes. She had a lot of small town in her and so, I guess, did I because we were very happy together.

We lived four years in Ashtabula, Ohio. Horses were being bought and sold at such a rate that we were able to put aside enough to buy a house —five hundred dollars down. At the last minute the seller refused to sign over the deed because he didn't think we could meet the installments. I got so mad I said that was just fine with us—we were planning to move away anyhow.

The next day I met a woman on the street I'd never cared much for. "And how is our prominent lawyer today?" she said to me.

(*Posing*)

Oh, fine, fine. I just got a big case.

"How nice. Here in Ashtabula?"

No-o-o. In Chicago.

"That's just lovely. When are you going to try it?"

Why—as a matter of fact—tomorrow.

The next day I took the early train to Chicago.

(*He starts the long walk across the stage to his office*)

I had to. If that woman had seen me on the streets, she'd have told the whole town I was a liar—

—which I was. So I came to—

(*Now in his office; with a glint of grim delight*)

Chicago! With straw in my hair, in a suit bought and fitted at the Ashtabula Hardware and Emporium. They tell me I've kept that look all my life. At the Scopes trial, some reporters were giving me a hard time. I told them "I spend as much on my clothes as you do—the only difference is I sleep in mine!"

> (*But now something else occurs to him, something that slows him. He looks at the Chicago skyline before he comes downstage, carrying the heavy weight of what he's just remembered*)

Chicago.

I got to Chicago at the most shameful moment in the city's history . . . just after the people of that city had demanded and been granted the death by hanging of four men they called anarchists.

Of all the men whose side I did not get to stand by until it was too late, the ones I'm sorriest about are the Haymarket Anarchists.

It began with the Chicago strike of 1886, when company police shot seven workers outside the McCormick plant. A protest meeting was called in Haymarket Square. The meeting was peaceable.

> (*The stage gradually grows black except for the spotlight on* DARROW'*s haunted face*)

A little after ten it started to rain. The listeners drifted away. There were only a few hundred still in the square when Captain Bonfield, acting against the mayor's specific orders not to bring police to Haymarket Square that night, charged into the square at the front of 180 uniformed men.

"We are peaceable!" cried the speaker. The meeting was over. "We are peaceable!"

At that instant, from one of the buildings above the square, some lunatic—to this day no one

15

knows who—threw a dynamite bomb. It landed among the policemen. It killed seven policemen and wounded sixty more . . .

(The lights start back up: DARROW *sags for a moment under the weight of the memory)*

. . . and it killed the socialist movement and the eight-hour day as well.

Eight men were taken—editors, lecturers, printers —eight men accused not of throwing a bomb, but of committing the unpardonable crime of writing that capitalism was the source of poverty, misery, and crime

—and the state of Illinois charged them with conspiring with a man unknown, or men unknown, in a place unknown, in a manner unknown, to throw the bomb. . . . They presented evidence manufactured by the police . . . and during the trial the judge admitted into evidence articles that the defendants had written and told the jury that if they believed these articles had influenced the man who threw the bomb, they were justified in convicting the defendants of murder.

Four of the eight were hanged. One, Louis Lingg, the youngest, killed himself in prison by biting down on a dynamite percussion cap and blowing his head off. Three were sentenced to long terms.

And the people of Chicago pronounced themselves satisfied.

Still—

—Chicago was an extraordinary place. It was life and excitement for me—new people and ideas, good talk and debates—and good friends like the great John Peter Altgeld who helped me get a job with the city as Special Assessments Attorney.

I didn't know what it meant, either, other than it meant sixty dollars a week.

I worked four years for the city of Chicago. I went up against the railroads quite a few times on right-of-way litigations and generally managed to lick 'em, so one day the Chicago and North Western came to me with an offer of a good job as their general attorney. I frankly wasn't sure—my thoughts on life didn't equip me for that sort of work—but Altgeld thought I should take it and finally I did. It helped us buy a nice home on the North Side where I hoped Jessie would be happy.

> (*Hesitates, then with a look at the apartment*)

She wasn't, really. The big city . . . new friends . . . new ideas . . . She felt it wasn't what she'd bargained for—and of course it wasn't. She grew not to like to do things. . . .

> (*Brooding, thinking he ought to say more. He crosses to the apartment*)

Did you have a nice day, Jess? Did you get out of the house? It was beautiful down by the lake.

I worry about you, cooped up in the house with Paul all day long. You could take him into the park in his carriage. . . .

No, 'course you don't, if you don't want to.

> (*Defeated, down, he turns away from the apartment*)

It wasn't one-sided, of course. It never is. For my part—among other things—I wasn't home much. I served the railroad all day—settling claims, representing them in court—and nights I went out with John Altgeld and my other new friends, freethinkers mostly, and talked law and books and politics till dawn.

I worked two years for the Chicago and North Western.

Then, in 1894, Eugene V. Debs took his railway union out in support of the Pullman strikers and struck every railroad in the country, including the one I was working for. And I had to choose sides.

George Pullman, the sleeping-car man, had built a brand-new town out of five hundred acres of Illinois prairie to house his workers. An extraordinary place. Listen to how he described it:

(Reading from a pamphlet he takes off his desk)

"Bright beds of flowers and green velvety stretches of lawn dotted with parks and pretty water vistas . . . homes filled with light . . . a town where all that inspires to cleanliness of person and of thought is generously provided."

I almost bought a home there myself.

There was just one small thing I couldn't understand—why anyone living in this paradise, this Garden of Eden, would ever want to go on strike. Was it conceivable—was it barely possible—that in this pamphlet his own company had put out, Mr. Pullman had inadvertently left out a detail or two? I took a train down to see for myself.

(Starts to walk and look around, filled with wonder)

The main street was a vision: bright red flower beds . . . rows of tall green trees lining the walks . . . houses of neat red brick with trim lawns. Lovely.

Only—and this was curious—one street back from the main street, where the workers lived, the houses didn't have lawns. . . . They didn't have windows. . . . They had, at most, one faucet, for cold water, and that was in the basement where it was cheapest to run the pipes in. Three, four, five families crowded into each tenement, all using one toilet. In the entire town where "everything that inspires to cleanliness of person is generously provided," not one bathtub.

I spoke to some of the people who lived there—at least I tried to. They were afraid to talk. Every move they made was watched. Everything they said was reported back to the company. If a man talked of joining a union, he was fired that day. His family was thrown out of its home and his name was put on a blacklist that was sent to every railroad in the country.

And the wages. Eighteen ninety-four brought hard times. Skilled men who had been paid three dollars and twenty cents a day saw their wages cut until, after Pullman took out their rent money, all they had left to feed their families on was four cents a week.

But the price of food in the Pullman Company store, where their wives had to buy—that stayed the same.

Forty-three men asked permission to come in to tell Mr. Pullman their families were starving to death. They asked for and were given a firm promise they would not be discharged if they came in to talk. Mr. Pullman listened to the forty-three men, said there was nothing to discuss, told them his only duty was to his stockholders and that there was no reason to give the workers a gift of money—and the next day fired them all and put their families out on the street.

That's when the Pullman strike started and Gene Debs called out his railway workers in support. 'Course, it didn't take our government any time at all to choose sides. They got one injunction making it a crime for a man to go on strike, another for one man to suggest to another that he even consider going on strike.

> (*Now his head snaps around as he sees and hears something. He looks quickly right and left until he is sure and then, his eyes blazing with anger, strides toward the audience*)

But I never thought I'd live to see the day when the United States Government would call out armed troops against its own unarmed citizens on the streets of Chicago! Look at them! Thirty-six hundred of them, guns drawn, bayonets fixed, lined up against the strikers! Look at them!

> (*Calling loudly*)

Do you know what day this is?? It's the Fourth of July! Independence Day!

> (*The stage starts to go dark*)

At first, angry names . . . then fists and stones
. . . until at three-thirty in the afternoon the men
charged into the troops who were trying to dis-
perse them. The soldiers started shooting as they
came.

Seven strikers killed!

Nobody in the Army charged. Debs and his entire
executive board indicted for conspiracy to com-
mit murder! His own people's murder.

And I went into the office of my boss, Mr. Marvin
Hughitt, president of the Chicago and North
Western Railroad.

(Coming downstage)

Debs has asked me to defend him against you,
Mr. Hughitt. I can't find any reason except my
own selfish interest for turning him down, so I'm
going to do it. I don't believe in socialism, but I
do believe that the government's ownership of
railroads is better for the people than railroad
ownership of government.

(Turns toward the court)

Gene Debs. There may have lived some time,
some place, a kindlier, more gentle soul, but I
have never known him. In his jail cell the night
before he went on trial he said to me, "Go get a
good night's sleep, Clarence, and don't worry
about me. We'll come out all right. If not this time
—next time."

> *(The lights come up on the jury box
> and judge's bench as* DARROW *starts
> his summation)*

Gentlemen:

If a boy should steal a dime, a small fine would cover the offense. He could not be sent to the penitentiary. But if two boys plot to steal a dime but do not do it, then both of them could be sent to the penitentiary as conspirators. Not only could they be, but people are constantly being sent under similar circumstances.

This is an historic case which will count much for liberty or against liberty. Conspiracy, from the days of tyranny in England down to the day the railroads use it as a club, has been the favorite weapon of every tyrant. It is an effort to punish the crime of thought. *If there are still any citizens interested in protecting human liberty, let them study the conspiracy laws of the United States* which have grown until today no one's liberty is safe.

There is a conspiracy here, dark and damnable, and I want to say boldly to this court that someone is guilty of one of the foulest conspiracies that ever disgraced a free nation. If my clients are innocent, other men are guilty of entering the temple of justice and using the law, which was made to guard and protect and shelter you and me and these defendants, for the purpose of hounding innocent men to a prison pen. This is not the first time that evil men—men who are themselves criminals—have conspired to use the law for the purpose of bringing righteous ones to death or to jail!

> (*He steps back, done; when he has recovered . . .*)

They sentenced Debs to six months in the Wood-
stock jail. He got off easy. No other offense has
ever been visited with such severe penalties as
seeking to help the oppressed.

(Coming downstage)

They put him in a large cell made for six people.
Outside the barred windows was a garden of
beautiful flowers. In the cell with him was a simple mountaineer from the South who had done
nothing but give nature a chance to convert corn
into whiskey. He could not imagine why he was
there, any more than I can imagine why men
who think themselves civilized build cells. There
were three or four others in the cell, and there
was the atmosphere of a happy family, and so it
was, for the place was radiant with the sunshine
and kindness and love of Eugene V. Debs.

"This place is not so bad," he said to me. "I look
at that garden of flowers. There are bars in front,
I know, but I never see the bars."

*(A moment before he turns to his
office)*

After Debs, I didn't consider going back to work
for the railroad. Fortunately, labor felt as well
disposed towards me as I felt towards labor, and
for the next seventeen years I was to represent
them in most of their important cases.

This informal arrangement lasted, happily on both
sides I believe, until 1911, when I was retained
by the American Federation of Labor to defend
the McNamara brothers in the Los Angeles *Times*
bombing case. After that trial, organized labor

would never have anything to do with me. They called me a traitor to their cause and some men spat in my face as I walked from the courtroom.

But that was not for seventeen years. In the nineties I was practicing law in Chicago—mostly on the side of the weak, sometimes on the side of the strong, but never on the side of the strong against the weak. My practice was mostly criminal and labor, with some civil. I was happy in my work and felt useful.

Being a lawyer in Chicago in contact with malefactors of all types, I can tell you that the Illinois legislature was none too good in those days, either. I've never known the representatives to be any different excepting at a time of some great moral crusade, and then they are always worse.

In Chicago we had a lot of massage parlors that were being used as fronts for houses of prostitution. It got so bad that the word "massage" came to mean . . . you can imagine what it came to mean . . . and to give someone a "massaging" meant . . . I suspect you know what that meant too, without my spelling it out.

Just to interrupt myself for a minute here, I've always thought most lawyers, myself included, like to say more than is absolutely necessary. I remember one counsel who was defending a man charged with biting another man's ear off in a fight. There was only one witness, and when counsel got up to cross-examine, he said, "You mean you didn't actually *see* my client bite this other fella's ear off?"

"No, sir," said the witness, and counsel of course could've sat down right then—but he's bound and determined to ask one more:

"Well, if you didn't *see* my client bite the man's ear off, how can you be so all-fire sure he *did* bite the man's ear off?"

"Well, sir, I saw him spit it out."

Anyway, as part of this reform movement in Chicago, all the massage parlors were closed up, thereby preventing a lot of hard-working masseuses from earning a living. Their association sent a committee to me, asking if I'd get an injunction against their being closed down. Did, too. Got the ordinance revoked. On my way out of court, the State's Attorney nudged me and said, "Clarence, you gave the State a good massaging on that one."

After I went out on my own, I didn't have much trouble getting clients. One reason may have been I never charged a fee if a man couldn't afford to pay. A lawyer has to do a great deal of work for which he cannot hope to be compensated, and that's how it should be. All he can hope is that once in a while he'll get a client who can afford to pay.

Once a young man came into my office and asked me to defend him on a charge of robbery. He said he wanted to pay a fee but didn't have any money right then. He did expect he could raise some by that evening. I told him I thought he'd better get another lawyer. I didn't care to accept any money that had been stolen—

So recently.

Once I went to the Cook County Jail to speak to
the prisoners. I told them what I honestly believe:

(To the audience)

There is no such thing as crime as the word is
generally understood. If every man and woman
and child had a chance to make a decent, honest
living, there would be no jails and no lawyers and
no courts . . . and there *should* be no jails. If
you would wipe them out, there would be no
more criminals than now.

A guard asked one of the prisoners what he
thought about all that.

"Darrow's too radical," the man said.

(His smile fades)

I've told a lot of men what I thought they ought
to do in the course of my lifetime . . .

(The jury box)

. . . usually twelve at a crack. Sometimes they
had the good sense to listen to me; sometimes
they had the good sense not to. For years I'd
been telling everyone I could catch that they
ought to take the best friend I'd ever had, the
wisest, most independent, incorruptible man in
the world, John Peter Altgeld, and elect him governor of Illinois.

Damned if they didn't do it, too, in 1892.

It was commonly believed that his first official act
would be to pardon the Haymarket Anarchists.
Three of them were still alive then, still in jail.
I certainly believed it.

Well, it wasn't his first act, or his second, or even his hundredth. He said that when he could spare the time he would go over the case and do what he thought was right, but he must take his own time.

In the next weeks and months I made the suggestion to him again, not once but several times. He always eluded me.

(*A deep breath, a painful memory*)

Finally I went to him one last time. I told him that everyone expected it, that despite what others were saying, it wouldn't create hostility towards him, and that I and others could see no excuse for waiting. I will never forget how he turned to me, calmly and quietly, and said—

"I don't want to offend you or lose your friendship, but don't deceive yourself. If I conclude to pardon those men, it will not meet with the approval you expect. Let me tell you that from that day I will be a dead man."

He studied the case until he was sure—

Then he granted the pardon.

The second time Altgeld ran for governor was two years later. He lost, as he knew he would. He could never win an election after that, and the reason always was The Pardon. The newspapers fought him bitterly; but in the factories and the mills and the mines, he was worshiped almost as a god. Even though he couldn't govern the people any more, he could still serve them and fight for them—and he did, until the day he died.

(*Entering the courtroom*)

In the whole country no one has it worse than the Pennsylvania coal miners. Men who work underground in twelve-hour shifts, 365 days a year, without Thanksgiving or Christmas off. Men whose *ten-year-old daughters work in the mills next to the mines for three cents an hour!*

The president of the Philadelphia and Reading Coal and Iron Company tells us "They don't suffer—why, they can't even speak English!"

(DARROW *turns to him*)

You say you love children, sir? I have no doubt that you do. Just as the wolf loves mutton.

> (*The lights turn dark blue, suggesting that the entire stage is a coal mine —except for the spotlight on the witness stand, which* DARROW *now approaches*)

You're a breaker boy, Johnny McCaffery. That means they set you and a hundred others astraddle the chute and as the coal comes rushing down, you pick out the slate?

What would you say that takes, Johnny? Quickness? You have to be quick to pick the slate out . . . ? Quick not to lose a finger, or a hand, or an arm?

Has that happened to any of your friends? How many of your friends?

Do they feed you, Johnny, before they send you into the breakers?

Do they give you anything besides the one po-
tato to take down on your twelve-hour shift?

Do they let you see the sun, all day long?

Do they give you one day off, all year long?

You don't look very old to me. How old are you?

When will you be eleven? When's your birthday?

> (*He walks away, shaking his head in
> deep despair, before returning to the
> witness box*)

You mine anthracite coal, Mr. Griffiths? How
much do they pay you for that?

Two-dollars-and-a-half a week. That's for a
twelve-hour day, seven-day week?

What vein are you working in?

How is the air in there?

What do you mean, bad? Do you have headaches?

Now, sir, go on and describe the effect the bad
air has on you. The headaches and the eyes and
the lungs.

Did you ever go to a doctor?

Does the company have doctors for the men? Any
at all?

Have you asked them for a doctor?

And they wouldn't?

Now, I want to ask you about the time you lost
your leg. Did the company offer to buy you a
wooden one?

They acknowledged the accident had happened in the mine and still they wouldn't . . . ?

(The lights fade out on the witness stand as DARROW *turns to the audience for his summation)*

This demand for a decent life, for an eight-hour day at a decent wage, is not a demand to shirk work as is claimed in this case. Gentlemen of the Commission, there is only one standpoint from which you have the right to approach this question, and that is what will make the best man, the best American citizen, to build up a nation we will be proud of?

The laborer who asks for shorter hours asks for a breath of life; he asks for a chance to develop the best that is in him. It is no answer to say, "If you give him shorter hours he will not use them wisely." Our country, our civilization, our race is based on the belief that for all his weaknesses, there is still in man that divine spark that will make him reach upward for something higher and better than anything he has ever known.

(As he finishes, the lights come up in his living room. He slowly goes toward it)

It took the Commission over a month to hand down its findings. Soon after we'd come to Chicago I'd told Jessie I'd rather help the men get the eight-hour day than be elected President of the United States. Now that we'd finally won, there was no one to share it with.

For a long time Jessie and I had been drifting apart.

Now the house and Paul were all we had in common.

(*Sitting in his living room*)

All these years, Jess, we've been taking different roads. We're not at the same place any more.

No, of course, it's not all your fault. . . .

Is there any sense to thinking it could be different? After eighteen years?

I don't know—I may be making a mistake—but I feel I must have my freedom.

I'm sorry, Jess.

(*Comes downstage, far from his home*)

Now that I was alone, I found myself working harder than ever at things I cared about.

We'd made a beginning in Pennsylvania, but in the West there was open warfare between miners and owners. A man named Harry Orchard—as low a specimen as you'd ever want to see—killed the former governor of Idaho with a bomb and said Big Bill Haywood, the union man, had put him up to it. Idaho's new governor, Gooding, sent deputies, without a warrant, to Colorado in the dark of night, to kidnap Haywood and run him back to Boise for hanging.

(*Straightening*)

The United States Constitution may have guaranteed Haywood a fair trial. Governor Gooding *did* guarantee—his exact words—that Haywood would never leave Idaho alive.

31

Everyone in Idaho stood up and cheered. Everyone but the miners.

Eighty days the trial ran, eighty days of rage and vituperation and bitterness. The judge's daughter said it sounded like eighty days in an insane asylum. I know I felt like one of the inmates.

I took the side of Bill Haywood.

He was a big man, and the toughest I ever met. Totally honest, fearless, incorruptible, strong as an ox inside and out. A terrible temper and only one eye, just like a pirate. And no stranger to violence, either.

(Entering the court)

I do not mean to suggest the workingman has always been right. I know he is sometimes wrong; I know he is sometimes cruel and sometimes corrupt; I know he is often unreasonable and unjust.

(The fire comes back; the eyes blaze; to the jury)

But to hang Bill Haywood, or any man, on the testimony of Harry Orchard!

(The stage goes black except for one piercing, pitiless spotlight on the witness chair)

Harry Orchard! This self-confessed perjurer who robbed miners of their ore; who shot and killed a drunken man in a dark street; who tried to murder the governor of Colorado; a man who, by his own admission, blew up a railroad station, killing thirty men. This is the man on whose testimony you're asked to hang Bill Haywood.

(*The lights come up on* DARROW)

Gentlemen:

This murder was cold, deliberate, cowardly in the extreme, and if this man sitting in his office in Denver fifteen hundred miles away employed this miserable assassin to come here and do this cowardly work, then for God's sake, gentlemen, hang him by the neck until dead.

But I sometimes think I am dreaming in this case. I sometimes wonder whether here in Idaho or anywhere in the country a man can be placed on trial and lawyers seriously ask to take the life of a human being upon the testimony of Harry Orchard. For God's sake, what sort of a community exists up here that sane men should ask it? Need I come here from Chicago to defend the honor of your state?

There is no way to give Haywood back the eighteen months he has spent in the Boise jail. If a man is so insane that he wants to go out and work for the poor, as Haywood has, these are the wages that he receives today and which he has received since the time the first foolish man commenced to agitate for the upbuilding of the human race.

But, gentlemen, it is not for Bill Haywood alone that I speak.

I speak for the poor, for the weak, for the weary, for that long line of men who in darkness and despair have borne the labors of the human race. Their eyes are upon you twelve men of Idaho tonight. If you kill Haywood, your act will be applauded by many. In the railroad offices of our great cities . . . among the spiders of Wall Street . . . in every bank in the world, where men hate Haywood because he fights against the system on which the favored live and grow rich and fat . . . from all these you will receive blessings and unstinted praise.

But if your verdict should be "not guilty" in this case, there are still those who will reverently bow their heads and thank you twelve men for the life and reputation you have saved. Out on our broad prairies where men toil with their hands, out on the wide ocean where men are tossed and buffeted on the waves, through our mills and factories and down deep under the earth, thousands of men and women and children will kneel tonight and ask their God to guide your hearts!

> (*He finishes, exhausted again; he sinks into his chair*)

As the case was sent to the jury, a sympathetic reporter leaned over to me.

"Well, it takes twelve," he said.

"No," I told him. "It only takes one."

I knew that in Boise the best we could hope for was a hung jury.

Just before five o'clock in the morning an eavesdropper outside the jury room heard the jury take a poll and the foreman announce a vote of eleven to one. In Boise that meant eleven to one for conviction. He told the newspaper, which had an extra on the street in ten minutes.

Boise rose up in joy. The women came out for breakfast in their finest jewelry, the men in their gayest suits and ties. They were all waiting for that last stubborn juryman to listen to reason. Then the barbecue and picnic would start.

Finally the one gave in.

(*Stands*)

"Have you reached your verdict?"

"We have, your Honor."

"And what is the verdict?"

"Not guilty!"

Not guilty.

(*A moment of bewilderment, of relief and gratitude. And now the most difficult time of his life. How to begin?*)

I felt, now, that I had done my share of the fighting. It was not easy to go against the powerful forces of society in the courts, as I had been doing for so many years. I had fought through so many conflicts that I felt the need of rest. Also, in my own life, after years of loneliness, first with Jessie, then without her, I had met someone. Ruby was a newspaperwoman, a very good one. And she was redheaded and beautiful, and we fell in love.

Up to this time, I'd felt, along with a good many others, that getting married was like going into a restaurant with a friend. You order what you want, and then when you see what the other fella got, you wish you'd taken that.

35

I've always been a finicky eater.

I don't like spinach and I'm glad I don't because if I liked it, I'd eat it, and I just hate it.

I don't like shredded wheat, either, and I don't like anybody who does.

After Ruby and I got married, I think I would have been happy to spend the rest of my life with her in Chicago, not running all over the country looking for new fights to fight.

But then, in 1911, the Los Angeles *Times* building blew up, with twenty men killed, and Samuel Gompers of the A. F. of L. persuaded me I would go down in history as a traitor to their great cause if now, in the hour of their greatest need, I refused to take charge of the McNamara defense.

I told him I didn't want to take the case. I pleaded to be excused.

(*Then, in pain*)

As hard as it was to give him my yes, it would have been harder to say no. Ruby and I left for Los Angeles.

(*Quietly; he has no taste for this*)

Los Angeles—known to every workingman in America as "the scabbiest town on earth." The Los Angeles *Times* and its publisher, Harrison Gray Otis . . . they ran the town. They fought the unions and they always won. Always.

Otis was a man to reckon with—a big, loud man with a walrus moustache, a goatee, and military bearing. He looked like Buffalo Bill or General Custer. He was a holy terror to work for. There were some who found things not to admire in Mr. Otis. I seem to remember that Hiram Johnson, the distinguished United States Senator from San Francisco, was one of them. . . .

(From a file on his desk)

"In the city of San Francisco" . . . this is Johnson speaking . . . "we have drunk to the very dregs of infamy; we have had vile officials; we have had rotten newspapers. But we have nothing so vile, nothing so low, nothing so debased, nothing so infamous in San Francisco as Harrison Gray Otis. He sits there in senile dementia with gangrened heart and rotting brain, grimacing at every reform, chattering impotently at all things that are decent, frothing, fuming, violently gibbering, going down to his grave in snarling infamy. He is one thing that all California sees when they look at anything disgraceful, depraved, corrupt, crooked, and putrescent—that is Harrison Gray Otis."

Otis could give as good as he got. According to the *Times*, union men were never anything but cutthroats, assassins, thieves, lunatics, anarchists and swine.

No union man was ever employed by the *Times*, in any capacity.

"This is war," Otis said, and he was right. These were years of hard and bitter fighting—until in the early hours of October 1, 1911, there was an explosion in an alley adjoining the *Times* plant. The explosion started a terrible fire in which twenty men—printers, machinists, compositors— were trapped and burned to death.

Before the ashes had cooled . . . before anyone could know what had caused the explosion . . . Harrison Gray Otis printed this in his paper . . .

(From his files; quietly)

"O you anarchic scum, you cowardly killers, go look at the ruins wherein are buried the calcined remains of those whom you murdered. . . ."

A man named Ortie McManigal was arrested on another charge. To save himself, he told the police that two good friends of his—James B. and John J. McNamara, brothers and leaders of the Structural Iron Workers Union—had put the bomb in the alley at the *Times.*

At the time the charge was made, John was in Indiana, James was in Illinois. Los Angeles sent men in the dark of night—it was the Haywood case in Idaho all over again—to kidnap them and rush them back for trial.

History repeats itself. That's one of the things wrong with history.

I came to the jail to meet my clients for the first time. James was twenty-eight, lean, with a bright gleam in his eye and a touch of the poet. John was twenty-seven, with a strain of Irish melancholy. He had studied law. I liked them both, right from the start.

That day I began to assemble a staff and start the months of preparation necessary for the defense. Every ounce of energy and devotion I had, I put into this case. I went to lengths I had never gone before, tracking down every possible piece of evidence, every witness, all across the country. We even hired a detective, Bert Franklin, to investigate each prospective juror.

When I started, I was sure of only one thing:

All labor throughout the country was convinced absolutely that the McNamaras were innocent.

Every union in the country contributed to the defense. Thousands of letters came to our office from workmen who wanted to make a small contribution from their savings.

But . . .

(*In pain*)

. . . the deeper I got into the case, the more it became unmistakably clear to me:

The McNamara brothers *had* planted the bomb at the *Times*.

Everything Ortie McManigal said they had done, they had done. And they had left a trail behind them a mile wide. And the state would surely hang them.

"Why?" I asked James. *Why?*

He wouldn't answer at first. Finally he said—

"There was a labor parade. The police beat up some of the boys. The next morning the *Times* praised those cops for their heroic work. It was more than I could stand. . . ."

(DARROW's *confidence is shaken, his face haggard*)

I didn't know what to do. I could not bear the thought of their hanging but I didn't know how to prevent it. I did not know what to do.

And then . . . it seemed barely possible that despite all the bitterness in Los Angeles, if the brothers admitted to everything before the trial, perhaps I could persuade the prosecution to allow them to plead guilty and go to jail.

I decided to try. I couldn't tell anyone, even Gompers, for fear of jeopardizing the negotiations.

After weeks of discussions—discussions with the prosecution, discussions with the McNamaras, discussions with Harrison Gray Otis—we were able to conclude an agreement that saved the brothers' lives. Full confessions. Life in prison for James McNamara. Fifteen years for John.

The negotiations were completed so late, the jury lists had already been selected.

And still, no one knew what we—what I—had done.

The day the trial was to open in Los Angeles, tens of thousands of our friends staged a parade. They cheered me all the way to the courtroom. I had to push my way through the crowd of well-wishers to get inside. Here, like in every city in the land, workingmen proudly wore their badges: McNamaras Not Guilty!

> (*A hush comes over the room; the light is on* DARROW *alone; he turns slowly, heavily, toward the bench*)

May it please the court, our clients wish to change their plea from not guilty to guilty.

(A long, despairing beat)

In the crowded courtroom, people would not believe what they had heard. Then—some wept. Some stood up, shaking. Men screamed in anger. All labor, all people who had believed in the McNamaras with all their hearts, had been told without warning they were wrong. They felt betrayed. Many felt that *I* had betrayed them.

(The lights start to dim over DARROW's *gaunt, drawn face)*

It was a long time before the great room emptied. I went out with the rest. It was growing dark. A few streetlights were turned on. McNamara buttons lay where they'd been thrown, in the gutter. Billy Cavanaugh, who was a policeman and still my friend, came to my side. He was alarmed by the people shaking their fists and calling me traitor and he took my arm.

"Come with me," he said.

I wasn't brave, but I looked him in the face and said, "No, Billy. I'll go down the street with the crowd. I've walked with them when they cheered me. I'll go back the way I came."

(He exits as the stage goes black)

INTERMISSION

ACT TWO

The only set changes are in the lights in the office and apartment, which have gone from gas to electric; and in the apartment, where there is evident brightening—lighter colors, chintz, more cheer.

DARROW *enters, subdued, to stand at the defense table, his fingertips resting lightly on the back of one of the two chairs. Looking down at the empty chair without focusing . . .*

DARROW:

Two days after the McNamara trial, before I could leave Los Angeles to return to my home and my friends in Chicago, I was myself arrested and indicted on two counts of trying to suborn— to bribe—to fix—the McNamara jury.

(*A lonely moment before . . .*)

One of my associates had hired Bert Franklin, a detective and former investigator for the Los Angeles District Attorney, to investigate prospective jurors in the McNamara trial. He did more than investigate them. He offered five of them bribes

43

—to bring in a verdict of not guilty or, if that was not possible, to hang the jury. There's no doubt about what Franklin did; he was caught by five Burns detectives as he stood on the corner of Third and Los Angeles streets in broad daylight, giving Lockwood a five-hundred-dollar down payment.

I was standing across the street at the time and saw him do it.

For weeks Franklin wouldn't say who he was acting for, if anyone. He did say that I hadn't anything to do with it or any knowledge it was being done.

Then Franklin was put on trial. He pleaded guilty and was let off with a fine. After that was settled, he told the grand jury I had given him the money, told him who to bribe and how and with how much. And so I was indicted.

I was on trial for three months—ninety-two days —longer than Big Bill Haywood, longer than Debs, longer than any man I'd ever defended. Joseph Ford from the District Attorney's office opened the trial by calling me a coward in court. He said I had corrupted some of the best men in Los Angeles. He said I had sacrificed John McNamara to save myself. He called my conduct viler than anything Judas or Benedict Arnold had ever done. He told the jury that since I had written there was no such thing as crime, I had encouraged the McNamaras to kill innocent men and therefore it was Darrow and not the McNamaras who had murdered the twenty men at the *Times.* He called me, then and throughout the trial, liar and perjurer.

(*Grim*)

I don't suppose I've ever in my life wanted to see anybody meet his maker before the appointed day, but there may've been one or two obituary notices I've read with approval.

(*It takes time and a deep breath for his cold anger to dissipate*)

I doubt I could have faced this trial without Ruby, who was at my side every moment, the entire time, in court and out. It was as hard on her as on me. I think what made it particularly difficult was that we were alone in a city without many friends, and most of those we had thought I was guilty. Even Billy Cavanaugh—

Even my old friend Billy Cavanaugh, the policeman, said, "Mr. Darrow, why did you have to go down to that corner and let yourself get caught? Why didn't you send me? You know you could trust me. I'd have watched Franklin for you."

(*Entering the court*)

When Judge Hutton called the case of "The People Against Clarence Darrow," my lawyer, Earl Rogers, stood as I had so many times and said, "Ready, your Honor," then I guess he had to touch me on the shoulder and say, "Clarence, you're supposed to stand, too—you're the defendant."

(*The bleakest moment of all; but again he recovers*)

Of course, I took an active part in my own behalf, especially in the cross-examination of Franklin:

45

(*He whirls to confront the witness box*)

Mr. Franklin!

You say that on October fifth I suggested to you that we had better take care of the jury and the next day said it was time to work on Bain and gave you a check for a thousand dollars.

If I was sending you out to bribe a prospective juror, would I give you a check that could be traced back or would I give you cash? If I wanted prospective jurors bribed, would I send you out, my chief investigator whose every move was being watched by Burns's operatives, or would I have imported a stranger for the dirty work? Would I send you on this bribery expedition when I knew that you had worked for the District Attorney's office for years?

If you didn't tell me where the bribe was to be passed, how would I know where to go to check on you? If I knew you were passing a bribe there, would I let myself be seen in the vicinity? Would I have picked one of the busiest corners in Los Angeles? Would I have crossed the street to talk to you, when I saw Detective Browne walking right behind you?

Or are all these things details in a gigantic conspiracy to destroy as many of labor's leaders and defenders as possible? Or is your entire testimony against me the price the District Attorney made you pay to keep yourself out of prison?

(*The light fades out on the witness stand, extinguishing Franklin; and as*

DARROW *crosses over—comes up again on the jury box. He has ended high; he starts low*)

Gentlemen of the jury . . .

I am a stranger in a strange land, two thousand miles away from home and friends.

I think I can say that no one in my native town would have made to any jury any such statement as was made of me by the District Attorney in opening this case. I will venture to say he could not afterward have found a companion in Chicago except among crooks and detectives if he had dared to open his mouth that way.

But here I am, in his hands. Think of it! In a position where he can call me a coward—and in all my life I never saw or heard so cowardly, sneaky, and brutal an act as Ford committed in this courtroom before this jury.

In examining you before you were accepted as jurors, the District Attorney asked you whether, if I should address you, you would be likely to be carried away by sympathy. You won't be if you wait for me to ask for sympathy. I have never asked sympathy of anybody, and I am not going to ask it of you twelve. I would rather go to the penitentiary than ask for sympathy.

But if I am going to the penitentiary, it will be a great solace to me in the long days of my confinement to think you used a little common sense in this case and were not carried away by Ford. Does it look like a case of jury bribing? Or does it look like something that was framed up? Franklin swears he believed Yonkin, Smith, Underwood, and the man Lockwood were honest and incorruptible—and he goes forth to bribe them.

What else does Franklin do? He puts five hundred dollars in his pocket and rushes off to bribe Bain, only Bain was out, so he runs over to see one of the neighbor's wives and leaves his card. Here's a detective for you! Why, he's got Sherlock Holmes faded. He's got Burns beaten forty ways. And you gentlemen are expected to stand for it. No, I am to stand for it. All you do is return the verdict; I stand for it.

I have said about all I care to about Franklin. I have said enough. I have said too much.

All I am asking you, gentlemen of the jury, is to consider his story. Is it reasonable or is it absurd? Lord! This court ought to adjourn until Monday morning and try this case with the insanity cases. Leave out the moral question. Leave out the tradition of a profession that I have followed for thirty-five years. Would I take that chance with these gumshoe men everywhere, their eyes on everyone connected with this case, detectives over the town thick as lice in Egypt?

Gentlemen, don't ever think that your own life or liberty is safe; that your own family is secure; don't ever think any human being is safe when, under evidence like this, I, with some influence and some respect, am brought here and placed in the shadow of the penitentiary.

I know my life. I know what I have done. My life has not been perfect; it has been human, too human. I have tried to help in the world. I have not had malice in my heart. I have done the best

I could. I ask you to save my liberty, and my name.

> (*The lights dim on the jury and come up on the defense table, where* DAR-ROW *now goes. Quietly, with only a short break—*)

The jury was out only thirty-four minutes before they came in. I thought they wanted instructions from the judge. But the foreman, Williams, stood up and said he had a verdict and he smiled and called out, "Not Guilty."

Ruby was at my side, and we hugged and kissed.

The first person to get to us was Judge Hutton, who ran down from the bench and embraced me.

I shook the hand of each juror and hundreds of others who gathered round. It was more than two hours before we could get out of court.

I've said I felt like a stranger in Los Angeles. Well, that wasn't so true by the end of the trial. Many people were very kind to me. One was Senator William Borah of Idaho, who had prosecuted the Haywood case which I had defended. In the middle of my own trial, someone said to him that since I'd bribed the McNamara jury, I'd probably done the same with Haywood and that's how we'd won—but Borah said, "No, Darrow didn't bribe those jurors. He just frightened them to death."

Another was a man I'd never met, Mr. Fred D. Gardner of Hot Springs, Arkansas.

> (*He takes two telegrams out of a pocket*)

While my trial was still going on, Mr. Gardner sent me this telegram:

I NOTICE FROM THE DAY'S PAPERS THAT YOU HAVE EXHAUSTED YOUR LAST DOLLAR IN YOUR DEFENSE. YOU HAVE SPENT YOUR WHOLE LIFE TRYING TO SEE THAT THE POOR GOT A SHOW. NOW YOU SHALL HAVE EVERY CHANCE THE LAW AFFORDS TO PROVE YOUR INNOCENCE. IF YOU WILL WIRE ME THE AMOUNT YOU REQUIRE, I WILL SEND IT TO YOU.

I wired him back that his kindness was so great I could hardly understand it—but yes, my condition, my need, is as you state it. I don't know your circumstances, Mr. Gardner, and whether I ought to let you

The next day he wired me again.

MAILING CHECK TODAY. WILL SEND MORE IF NECESSARY. CHEER UP, TAKE HEART, AND PROVE TO THE WORLD THAT YOU ARE INNOCENT. YOU MUST NOT BE LOST TO THE POOR OF THIS NATION ON ACCOUNT OF THE LACK OF A FEW PALTRY DOLLARS TO MAKE A LEGITIMATE DEFENSE.

Signed . . . Fred D. Gardner.

In a few days I received his check for a thousand dollars and one for two hundred dollars from his wife, from her own savings.

I found out later that Mr. Gardner was not a wealthy man, and in his small factory he had had serious labor difficulties and was unsympathetic to unions. But he never thought of any of that.

(*Putting the telegrams away*)

He was a wonderful man.

(Finally he goes to his office, taking his time. He looks around, remembering)

I was gladder than you know to get home to Chicago, even if for a long time Chicago didn't feel so glad to have me. That's how things are sometimes—

—the charge hangs on after the acquittal. It took some people many years to forget what they thought I'd done and trust me with their cases. Some never forgot. Of all the clients I'd represented before my own trial—corporate, labor, individual—none ever asked me to represent him again. It looked like my lawyering days were over.

And then a very kind young man named Peter Sissman, who'd apprenticed in my old firm in the 1890s, asked me to come in as his partner. I told him I didn't have the heart for it, that I was through with the law. He said I had to—that if I didn't, it would be a tacit admission of guilt. I told him I couldn't bring him any business. He said that was all right, too.

I was with Peter Sissman three months before I got my first case, a year before I started pulling my weight. We had a mostly criminal practice, and I met and defended some unpopular people, unfortunate souls . . . murderers, alleged or in fact. I never hesitated to defend a man accused of murder, if only to prevent a second murder, by the state.

(Coming downstage)

One was Isaac Bond, who was a Negro.

A white nurse was murdered in a lonely spot near Chicago. She was found almost naked . . . her body badly mutilated. She had last been seen walking on the road in the company of a tall Negro. The police went through their files of ex-convicts and found a picture of Isaac Bond, who had served four years in a Missouri prison on a charge of killing a white man in self-defense. Bond was a Negro and he was tall; with no further connection than that, his picture was printed in the papers. Bond saw it and went right to police headquarters where he gave a detailed report of the work he had been doing in Gary, Indiana, the night of the murder. The police locked him up right then. I went to Gary and interviewed all the men who'd seen Bond at work that night. I showed the jury that there was not the slightest shred of evidence to connect him to the murder, which had taken place miles away.

The best he could get was a life sentence.

The jury brought in a verdict not against Bond but against the horrible crime; Bond just happened to be the first one accused of it. And of course he was a Negro.

Some years later I took the case to the pardon board and am convinced they thought I was right. One even said he was satisfied that I was but did not dare touch it because the killing was so brutal and revolting.

Isaac Bond served ten years in prison, where he contracted tuberculosis and died.

These were hard times for unpopular people—

(*Entering the court*)

—Red-baiting . . . Palmer raids . . . witch-hunts. Government and newspapers telling people to mob, jail, and kill dissenters—

Like the sixteen Chicago Communists guilty of the crime of—talk—

—And the secretary of the Rockford branch of the Communist Labor Party, accused of using the entire resources of his party's treasury—the entire thirty cents—to overthrow the Government of the United States—

—The eleven Italian anarchists in Milwaukee—

(*To the jury*)

—who may have had the bad taste to call this country a jail and our President a pig; but, gentlemen, those are errors of judgment rather than transgressions against the legal structure. I shall not argue to you whether the defendants' ideas are right or wrong. I am not bound to believe them right in order to take their case, and you are not bound to believe them right in order to find them not guilty. But if this jury should make it harder for a man to be a rebel, you would be doing the most you could for the damnation of the human race.

(*Coming downstage*)

We lost most of these political cases in court and lost them again on appeal. But every now and again one judge would agree with us in dissent. If there's only one man to state the case for freedom, maybe that's all it takes. One.

In addition to law, I did some lecturing and debating on the Chautauqua circuit after we got back to Chicago. It helped with the expenses those first few years and eventually I grew to enjoy it as much as anything I did.

I always took the anti-side in debate. I liked the feeling of getting to my feet after my opponent had gotten his ovation and facing an audience of five hundred or a thousand people who were waiting for me to fall on my face—

—And then I liked trying to turn some of those people toward my way of thinking or at least make them ask themselves a question or two.

Should the United States have Prohibition? Take out of this world the men who have drunk, down through the past, and you would take away all the poetry and literature and practically all the works of genius the world has produced. What kind of a poem do you suppose you would get out of a glass of ice water?

Does man have an immortal soul? Once I was debating a man who got carried away and told the audience, "I am the master of my fate; I am the captain of my soul."

Captain of his soul, hell—he wasn't even deckhand on a raft.

Is Life Worth Living? No—

—Although I see a fine-looking woman in the fourth row there who's a good argument for the other side.

(With a smile)

One of the things I believed in all these years which was even less popular than the labor movement was—Free Love. It was commonly said that I spoke for it in the abstract—and also that I believed in it in the particular on suitable occasions —though the plain fact of the matter is that after Ruby and I got married she kept a close eye on me. Anyhow, rumors about philandering don't do you nearly as much harm as the people who spread them would like to believe. The only time I was seriously concerned about this sort of thing was once when I was told that a District Attorney had a picture—which may have been tricked up —of me leaving a beautiful widow's house at dawn and that he planned to use it against me in court. But a friend said not to let it bother me. My enemies would believe the worst of me, even without the photograph, and my friends would know it was a fake. They would know that if I'd spent the night in the home of a beautiful woman, I wouldn't have left at dawn. I'd have stayed for breakfast.

I've often told young men starting out in business not to make acquaintances, but to make friends. Acquaintances are of little value unless you want to run for office, and I know that each of you has a higher ambition than that.

When I was a little boy growing up on the farm outside Kinsman, Ohio, I was taught to believe as an article of faith that *any* little boy, growing up anywhere in America, could eventually, someday, hope to become President of this great land and all its people.

Now I'm beginning to believe it.

Being a lawyer, on the other hand—that's a different kettle of fish—a high art requiring sophisticated discipline and the most rigid application of scientific principles.

How to pick a jury, for example:

If a Presbyterian enters the jury box and carefully rolls up his umbrella, let him go. He is cold as the grave; he knows right from wrong, though he seldom finds anything right. Get rid of him with the fewest possible words before he contaminates the others.

If possible, Baptists are more hopeless than Presbyterians and the sooner they leave the better.

Methodists are worth considering; they are nearer the soil. If chance sets you down between a Methodist and a Baptist, you'll move toward the Methodist to keep warm.

Either a Lutheran or a Scandinavian is unsafe, but if both in one, plead your client guilty and go down the docket.

I've never been much for organized religion or anything else that tells people what they ought to believe and what will happen to them if they don't. The fear of God or anything else is not the beginning of wisdom. Better to have doubt. Doubt leads to investigation, and that's the beginning of wisdom.

Still, I'm a lawyer, so I'm supposed to check these things out for myself. Ruby and I took a vacation in Palestine to see where it all began. We met an Arab boatman there who offered to row us out to the spot where Jesus walked on the water. All he wanted for this was fifteen dollars. No wonder Jesus walked.

(*Pleasantly, enjoying himself*)

The most religious people, the most righteous believers of all, are of course the Fundamentalists, who believe that every word in the Bible is literally true and don't want the schools or anyone else teaching anything different. Noah got two of every species of animal on the ark, including a million insects.

(*Here he stops to scratch himself innocently*)

Joshua made the sun stand still so the day could be lengthened and he could finish the battle. Balaam's ass spoke to him, probably in Hebrew. Many asses have spoken, and doubtless some in Hebrew, but they have not been that breed of ass.

(*And, stripping off his jacket like a barroom fighter—*)

William . . . Jennings . . . Bryan.

Welcome to Tennessee, sir.

(*Approaching the stand*)

You have given considerable study to the Bible, haven't you, Mr. Bryan? You have written and published articles on the Bible almost weekly for fifty years. . . .

Do you believe that everything in the Bible should be interpreted literally?

So when you read that the whale swallowed Jonah, you accept that literally?

Was it the ordinary run of whale, or made especially for that purpose? Aaah, I see. It was a miracle.

You believe Joshua made the sun stand still?

So you also believe at that time the sun went around the earth? No? Then it must have been the earth he made stand still.

Have you ever pondered what would naturally happen to the earth if it stood suddenly still? Don't you know it would have been converted into a molten mass of matter? Don't you care?

Do you believe the story of the flood? When was the flood? About 2348 B.C. That's according to Bishop Usher's calculations, and you accept them? All right. You believe that all living things that were not contained in the ark were destroyed. So that 4,273 years ago—

(*Making elaborate calculations with pencil and paper*)

—taking the 1,925 years since the Bible and adding them to the 2,348 years going back to the flood—

—So that 4,273 years ago there was not a living thing on the earth, excepting the people on the ark and the animals on the ark and the fishes?

Any idea who Noah threw the rope to when he docked the ark?

Do you believe the first woman was Eve? Do you believe she was literally made out of Adam's rib?

(*Irritatingly—yes*)

Did you ever discover where Cain got his wife? The Bible says he got one, doesn't it? Were there other people on the earth at that time? There were no others but Cain got a wife. . . .

When the Bible says "the morning and the evening were the first day," does that mean anything to you? Were those twenty-four-hour days? No? Any idea how long they were? Do you believe the sun was made on the fourth day? Then how could you distinguish the evening from the morning of the first three days, without any sun? The Bible does. Your Bible does. Doesn't that bother you?

(*Right in Bryan's eye*)

You say my argument's going in one ear and out the other? I'm not surprised—there's nothing in between to stop it!

(*He walks away, angry, to get his jacket . . .*)

If today you can take a thing like evolution and make it a crime to teach it in the public schools, tomorrow you can make it a crime to teach it in the Church. And the next session you may ban books and newspapers. If you can do the one, you can do the other.

(*. . . but he can't stay mad; he's enjoyed himself too much*)

A lot of people were sure that as I got older and closer to my final exams, I'd get religion. Even after the Monkey Trial.

(He smiles, a little tired, and now somehow—is it an illusion?—he looks a little older. Maybe a stoop is evident. Maybe he speaks more softly)

I never did. I still believe that when I die there'll be nothing left over, neither heaven nor hell. Ruby has a slightly different point of view. She believes there is a heaven and a hell, but it won't make any difference which one I go to—I'll have so many good friends in both places.

Once, after a debate in which I'd said I didn't believe in an afterlife, a nice blond lady asked me if there wasn't anything I did believe in.

I used to believe in blondes.

But that was a long time ago.

Ruby and I have had a good life since we married thirty years ago. I've worked all over the country, but I've never gone anywhere to try a case without Ruby, and I wouldn't, even if she'd let me.

My son Paul's president of his own company now. He has a wife and three little girls, and I see them every chance I get. I'd like to take credit for Paul's success, but the best advice I remember giving him was never to play in a no-limit poker game.

I don't look forward to death because I don't like to give up those I love, especially now that I have grandchildren, and I have lived so long I have formed the habit. But neither do I fear death, which at least brings rest and peace.

I have found that no one wants another life. We

all just want to go on living, which is quite a different matter.

Maybe someday we'll even be willing to let the other fellow live.

A committee came to me from the National Association for the Advancement of Colored People asking me to defend eleven Negroes in Detroit who were charged with murder. I told them I was tired after forty-eight years in the law and not mentally or physically fit. I knew I would go when I was making the excuses. I knew as soon as they told me about Dr. Ossian Sweet.

In the early days, Detroit and other northern cities were friendly to Negroes—but that was a long time ago. Now—you all know about the Chicago riots which began when a colored boy on a raft was washed to a white bathing beach, where men and boys of my race stoned him to death —120 people killed in those riots. Washington. St. Louis. Detroit. I'm not blaming Detroit. I'm saying what happened here.

Dr. Sweet bought a house, a nice house, at the corner of Charlevoix and Garland streets, in an all-white section. As soon as the neighborhood found he was a Negro, they banded together into a "Neighborhood Improvement Association" and made threats. Dr. Sweet asked the police for protection, which they provided, and then moved his wife and goods into the house. He took his two brothers and some friends with him.

He also took a number of rifles and a valise full of cartridges.

Dr. Sweet was a man of strong character. A white man does pretty well when he does what Dr. Sweet did. A white boy who can start in with nothing and put himself through college, study medicine, taking postgraduate work in Europe, earning every penny as he goes along, shoveling snow and coal, is some fellow. But Dr. Sweet had the handicap of the color of his face. And there is no handicap more terrible than that.

So Dr. Sweet moved into his new house. The first night a crowd gathered. They made some noise, but that was all. Inside the house nobody went to bed; they kept the lights off and looked out the windows all night.

The second night the crowd grew bigger and more boisterous. Some eight or ten policemen were stationed around the place but it seemed they were mainly ornamental. Then, at eleven o'clock, as the men in the house were standing at the window with guns, Dr. Sweet's brother drove up. The mob attacked him as he tried to make his way to the house, then rushed the house, throwing rocks as they came.

Shots were fired from the house into the street— where a white man, Leo Breiner, was killed. All eleven people in the house—Dr. Sweet, his wife and brothers and seven friends—were arrested on the spot and charged with murder in the first degree.

As you would expect, the feeling in Detroit ran strongly against them. There are not many colored people in America charged with killing white people who have lived to tell the tale.

I went to the Detroit jail to meet with Dr. Sweet. He was a young man, serious and quiet and attractive. He told me about that night—about the mob yelling, "Niggers! Get them! Get the Niggers!"—and the people rushing the house—"like a human sea" is how he described it—and the stones hailing against the house. "When I opened the door to let my brother in and saw the mob," he said, "I realized I was facing the same mob that had hounded my people through its entire history. In my mind I was confident of what I was up against. I knew what mobs had done to my people before."

(DARROW *nods—he knows too—as he walks into the courtroom*)

The legal problem was to show that the people outside the house constituted a mob which endangered the Sweets' lives.

The prosecution said they did not, that there were far too few of them to represent any danger. They presented so many eyewitnesses to testify that there hadn't been a mob that—

—the witnesses themselves were a mob. We were able to get the owner of a filling station to admit he had sold an unusual amount of gas that night . . . and a policeman who denied that there had been a mob to admit that he had run for reserves . . . and we told the court about the pounds of rocks that were found on the Sweets' front lawn the following morning.

But the real problem was to show that this was not a murder case but a case of race prejudice.

That meant the case could be won or lost in choosing the jury.

(*He starts to walk back and forth in front of the jury box, questioning each man*)

If we are to choose wisely, I have to know what you really feel about the Negro. Do you consider him as an equal? As a fellow American? Do you like him? Do you believe in him? Do you believe you could give him as fair and square a deal as you would a white man?

(*Finally he seems satisfied; he walks away from the jury, then turns back to them to begin his case . . .*)

My friend the prosecutor says, gentlemen, that this isn't a race question. Race and color have nothing to do with this case. This is a case of murder.

I insist that there is nothing but prejudice in this case; that if it was reversed and eleven white men had shot and killed a black while protecting their home and their lives against a mob of blacks, nobody would have dreamed of having them indicted. I know what I am talking about, and so do you. They would have been given medals instead. Ten colored men and one woman are in this indictment, tried by twelve jurors, gentlemen. Every one of you are white, aren't you? We haven't one colored man on this jury. We couldn't get one. One was called, and he was disqualified. You twelve white men are trying a colored man on race prejudice.

You need not tell me you are not prejudiced. I know better. We are not very much but a bundle of prejudices anyhow. We are prejudiced against other people's color, prejudiced against other men's religions, prejudiced against other people's politics, prejudiced against people's looks, prejudiced about the way they dress. We are full of prejudices. You can teach a man anything beginning with the child; you can make anything out of him, and he is not responsible for it.

My only hope, gentlemen of the jury, is this: that you are strong enough, and honest enough, and decent enough to lay it aside in this case and decide it as you ought to.

What do you think is your duty in this case? I have watched day after day these black, tense faces that now are looking to you twelve whites, feeling that the hopes and fears of a race are in your keeping.

Their eyes are fixed on you. Their hearts go out to you. Their hopes hang on your verdict.

> (*He finishes and steps back; after a long moment, to the audience . . .*)

The jury deliberated more than forty hours and finally reported they could not agree. The judge had to declare a mistrial.

We tried the case a second time. This time we won.

> (*Leaving the court, heading slowly toward his apartment*)

The world doesn't change without trouble, in some cases without disaster. There've been times when I wished I were either younger or older. If I were younger, I'd go to the South Seas. If I were older, I wouldn't care so much.

I don't go into the heart of the city much any more. I usually don't even leave the neighborhood. Ruby and I have lived for twenty-three years in this apartment and don't want to move. Now that Paul and his family are so close, we'll stay here the rest of our lives.

Every few days I get a letter from some friend asking why they never see me any more—whether they have in some way offended me. I answer, "No, nothing like that has happened; I am always glad to see my friends. I am only letting go of things in general. Of course, I shall come to see you soon," I say, "and will have you over to our house."

And I mean it, too. But next day the armchair lures me back to its depths, and by and by I gaze out the window down over the treetops of the park; the walk winds through the green velvety grass on toward the lake so blue and beautiful; I really don't feel like going anywhere today. Perhaps tomorrow I shall go and visit my friends. Perhaps.

I would feel better about my work if I could see any advance had been made in law since I was admitted to the bar more than fifty years ago; in science and mathematics the world has been made over new; even in religion there is an entirely modified and broader attitude. The whole material world has been made over, but the law and its administration have stood frozen and adamant, defying time and eternity and all the changes of our day and age.

You wonder what the compensations are? For me there has been one that has made it all worth while:

One hundred and two men I have defended have faced the death penalty and none has been hanged.

And none ever will be, because I would never dare to take another chance.

> (*He smiles softly and turns and starts to walk away from the courtroom— but after a few steps he stops and turns back, stricken, haunted*)

Unless—unless—unless I knew there was no other way.

Why did they kill?

Not for money, not for spite, not for hate.

They killed little Bobby Franks as they might kill a spider or a fly, for the experience.

They killed him because they were made that way.

Because somewhere in the infinite processes that go to the making up of the boy or the man, something slipped, and these unfortunate lads sit here hated, despised, outcasts, with the community shouting for their blood.

> (*He faces the bench in pain*)

Your Honor—when the public is concerned and demands a punishment, no matter what the offense, great or small, it thinks of only one punishment, and that is death. None of us are unmindful of the public, your Honor. I have stood here for three months as one might stand at the ocean trying to sweep back the tide. I hope the seas are subsiding and the wind is falling, and I believe they are, but I wish to make no false pretense to this court. The easy thing to do and the popular thing to do is hang Dickie Loeb and Babe Leopold. Men and women who do not think will applaud. The cruel and thoughtless will approve. But more and more fathers and mothers who are gaining an understanding and asking questions not only about these poor boys, but about their own—they will join in no acclaim at the death of my clients. They would ask that the shedding of blood be stopped.

Your Honor stands between the future and the past. I know the future is with me and what I stand for here. I am pleading for a time when hatred and cruelty will not control the hearts of men, when we can learn by reason and judgment and understanding that all life is worth saving, and that mercy is the highest attribute of man.

I feel that I should apologize for the length of time I have taken. This case may not be as important as I think it is. If I should succeed in saving these boys' lives and do nothing for the progress of the law, I should feel sad indeed. If I can succeed, my greatest reward and my greatest hope will be that I have done something to help human understanding, to temper justice with mercy, to overcome hate with love.

I was reading last night of the aspiration of the old Persian poet, Omar Khayyam. It appealed to me as the highest that I can envision. I wish it was in my heart, and I wish it was in the hearts of all.

> So I be written in the Book of Love,
> I do not care about that Book above;
> Erase my name or write it as you will,
> So I be written in the Book of Love.